PHONICS CONNECTIONS

At the Vet

by Amy Levin

I0894321

capstone classroom

A vet is a kind of doctor. Vets are doctors who help pets.

This little kitten is not fat. It sits on a scale. The kitten does not weigh much.

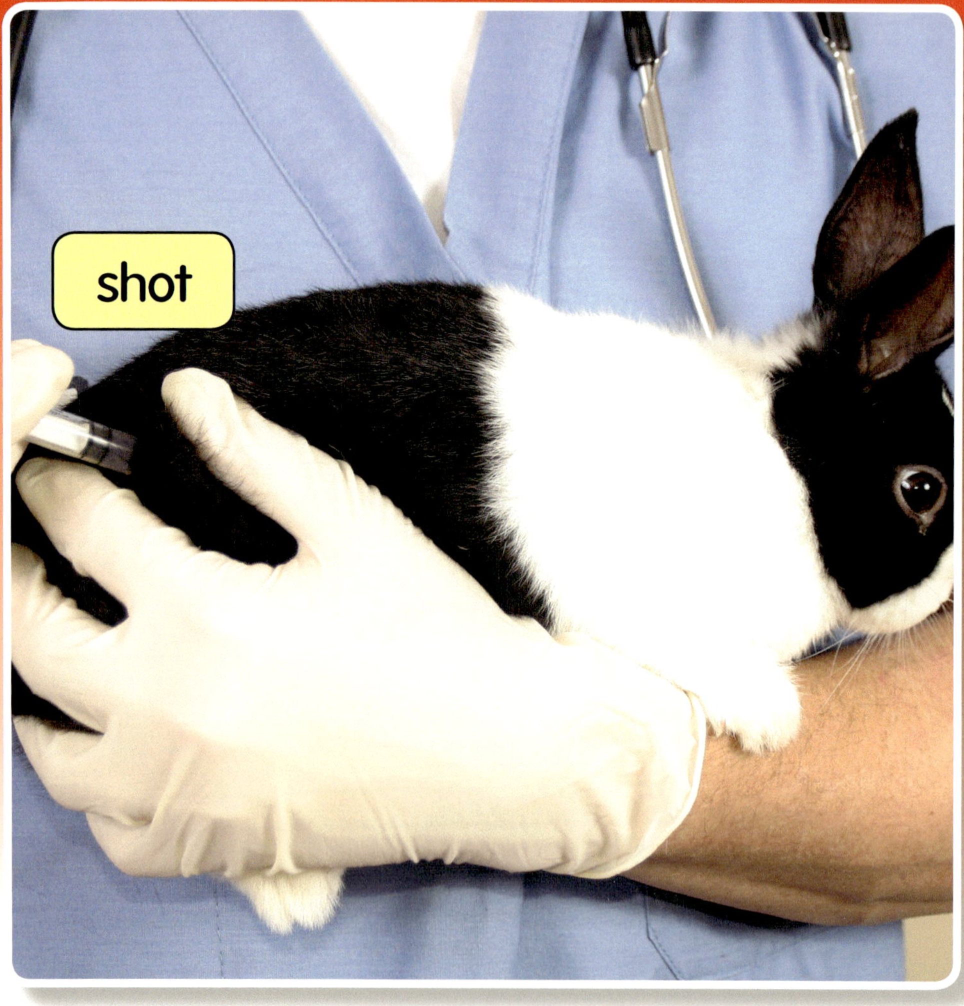

A black and white rabbit gets a shot.The shot will make it well.

A cat has a bad leg. It gets a cast.
The cat will feel better soon.

A dog had glass in its paw. The vet got it out. The dog's paw will now heal.

This pup is not sick. It does not need pills. The vet keeps it healthy.

A vet can help your pet. Stop in and visit the vet to keep your pet well.